Fashionable Clothes

Miriam Moss

Costumes and Clothes

Accessories
Children's Clothes
Clothes in Cold Weather
Clothes in Hot Weather
Fashionable Clothes
Hair and Make-Up
How Clothes Are Made
Sports Clothes
Theatrical Costume
Traditional Costume
Uniforms
Working Clothes

Some words in this book are
printed in **bold.** Their meanings
are explained in the glossary on
page 30.

First published in 1988 by Wayland (Publishers) Ltd
61 Western Road, Hove, East Sussex BN3 1JD, England.

Editor: Deborah Elliott

Designer: Joyce Chester

Cover: The pop trio 'Krush'. The two men are wearing trendy jeans and bomber
jackets and the woman in the middle is wearing fashionable BMX trousers and
leather boots.

British Library Cataloguing in Publication Data
Moss, Miriam
    Fashionable Clothes.
    1. Fashion
    I. Title   II. Costumes and clothes
    746.9′ 2

    ISBN 1-85210-100-8

Photosetting by Oliver Dawkins Limited, Burgess Hill, West Sussex
Printed in Italy by G. Canale & C.S.p.A., Turin
Bound in France by A.G.M.

Contents

Fashionable Clothes

Fashionable clothes are the particular styles that are thought to be the most up-to-date at any one time. All sorts of clothes have been considered fashionable at different times throughout history. For hundreds of years only the rich could afford to wear expensive, hand-made, fashionable clothes. They were responsible for changing the fashions. King Edward VII was so plump that he left the last button on his waistcoat undone — a habit that everyone copied and which became very

This model is wearing designer clothes at a Paris fashion show that will set new trends for the coming season.

Left **Princess Diana only has to appear in a new outfit at an official function and dress designers all over the world copy the style and make cheaper versions for sale in high street shops.**

There was a fashion 'revolution' in the mid 1970s when 'punk rock' burst on to the scene. The punk movement was an exciting and new type of youth fashion. People dyed their hair many different and unusual colours and wore clothes made from 'new' materials such as PVC. Many young people felt they could express their views on music, fashion and society through their style of dress.

fashionable at the time. Even today, people copy the clothes and hairstyles of members of the British royal family such as Princess Diana. Now cheap clothes are **mass-produced** in factories or imported from other countries, so most people can afford to dress fashionably if they choose to.

The kind of clothes we wear can tell other people what to think of us. They can make us look richer or poorer, younger or older, interesting, odd or even dull! Fashionable clothes are designed to please the wearer. Different styles are worn for different reasons. Punks wear clothes to attract attention and to make themselves deliberately stand out from the crowd. Their clothes express the distrust

and anger they feel at the society in which they live. People wearing casual, fashionable clothes do not want to attract attention — they want to appear 'in-step' with society. People wearing the same kind of clothes show others that they belong to a group who share similar beliefs and lifestyles. They may like the same kind of music or support the same sports team, for example.

Being aware of what is going on in the world can be reflected in our dress sense. Fashionable ideas are constantly changing. People, events and the **media** influence fashion. New, short-term trends come from the fashionable centres of the world like London, Paris, New York and Rome.

Fashion and Change

Changing shapes

Throughout history humans have wanted to change the natural shapes of their bodies. Often comfort has been sacrificed for a fashionable appearance. With the aid of whalebone, wood, leather, iron, starch and stuffing, various fashionable clothes have deliberately changed the body's natural

Left Can you imagine how uncomfortable it must have been to wear a head-dress such as this, worn in the eighteenth century? Clothes do not always become fashionable because they are practical to wear.

Below Notice how in the eighteenth century children's fashions were similar to those of adults.

silhouette. When it was fashionable to be large, hips were padded and widened and arms puffed out into huge **leg-o'mutton** shapes. Similarly, when slim, waif-like figures were in fashion, figure-hugging clothes became popular.

The rich and the powerful have always liked to wear the very latest fashions. In the past, they wore impractical fashionable clothes, like sleeves that dangled to the floor or enormously long points on their shoes, to show others that they did not have to do hard physical work. As these fashions were copied by ordinary folk, new fashions had to be invented to keep one step ahead. Sometimes kings and queens passed **sumptuary laws** forbidding poorer people from wearing, for example, gold braid or **ermine** fur!

The style, shape and length of fashionable clothes are continually changing. There have been many incredibly uncomfortable fashionable clothes. Elizabethans wore huge, stiff ruffs framing their heads. For years women wore suffocatingly tight corsets to make their waists look tiny. In the eighteenth century women wore **paniered** skirts that were sometimes 1.8 m wide. With these they were expected to wear towering hairstyles which were decorated with flowers, fruit, huge feathers and even model ships. In 1850 the **crinoline** was invented, allowing skirts to be enormous but not too heavy to wear. Finally the all-round fullness was gathered in at the back and the **bustle** became popular.

The bustle, panier and crinoline. These extraordinary frameworks were worn underneath women's skirts to change the shape of their bodies.

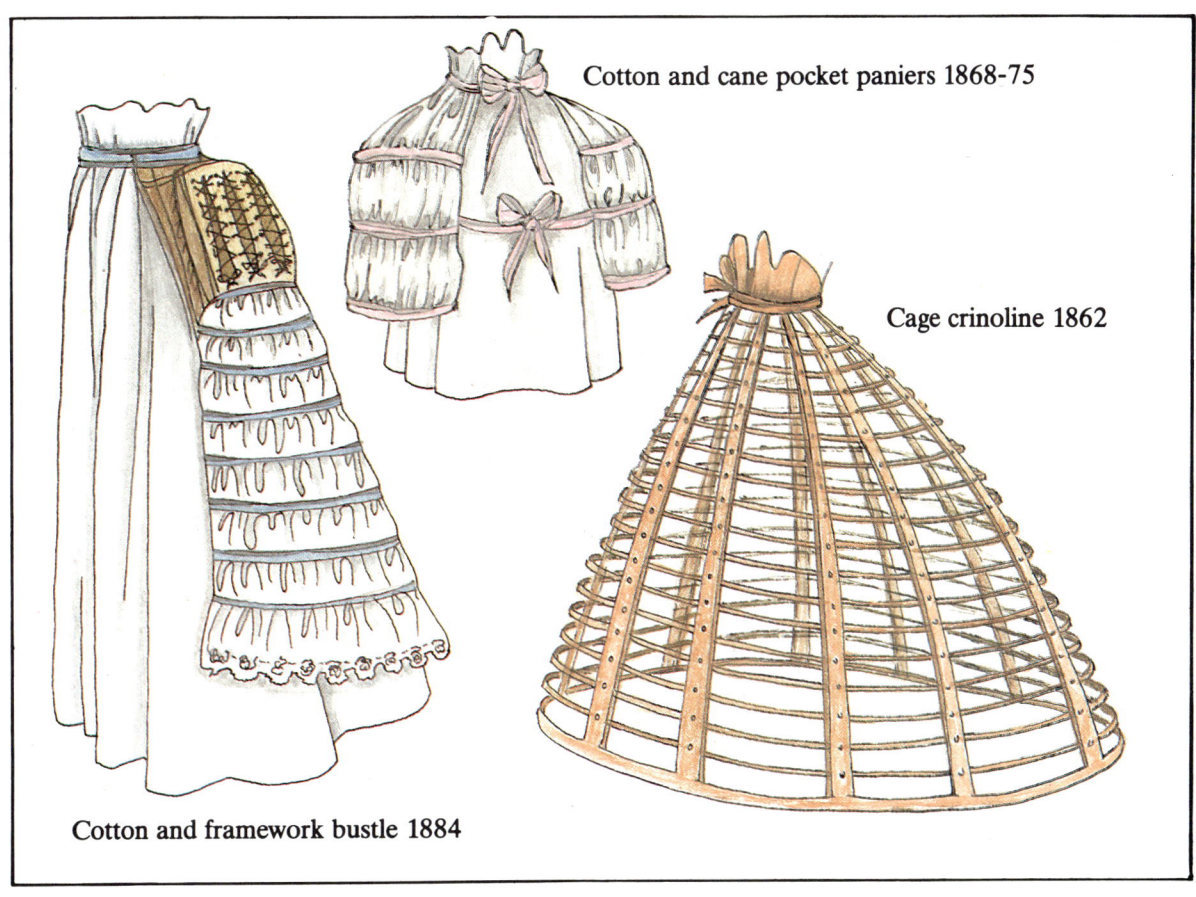

Cotton and cane pocket paniers 1868-75

Cage crinoline 1862

Cotton and framework bustle 1884

Changing times

Fashion is affected by historical events and changing ideas about behaviour and lifestyle. In the seventeenth century the **Puritans** believed that people would behave more sensibly if they did not attract attention to themselves and their bodies, so they wore dark, plain clothes.

Fashion is affected by war, revolution and hard times. Shortages of materials during the Second World War led to the plain 'utility' look which copied military uniform styles. Skirts were short and straight, using as little material as possible, and very little decoration. Women helping in the war effort needed practical clothes for doing physical work and so trousers for women became more fashionable.

Sometimes new generations of young people react against the ideas of their parents. In the 1960s the hippy style of dress was worn by people who did not want to copy their parents' lifestyles. They dressed in loose, colourful clothes, not the smart, formal styles of their parents.

Often one fashion brings another one with it. The slim **empire line** dresses that followed the huge skirts of the eighteenth century left no room for pockets, so carrying a handbag became fashionable. Early this century women cut their hair short and so cloche hats

The hippies of the late 1960s and early 1970s rebelled against the formal dress of their parents. Men began to wear their hair longer and both men and women wore bright, patterned clothes.

Left **A freer and more relaxed era followed the First World War. It was acceptable for women to show more of their legs. Women also cut their hair short and many wore small cloche hats.**

became the rage. When the mini skirt became fashionable, tights were designed to cover the legs. New movements like the **women's liberation movement** of the 1960s and 70s can also affect fashion. This particular movement directed fashion to unisex clothing, with styles that both men and women could wear. Inventions and historical events can also often affect fashion. Pierre Cardin, a famous French designer, brought in space age fashions following *Apollo 11*'s landing on the moon in July 1969. Many people wore 'moon boots' which were copied from those worn by the American astronauts.

In the 1960s the model Twiggy set a whole new trend in women's fashion. She was extremely thin and wore short dresses and skirts. Unfortunately, many women hoping to look 'fashionable', like Twiggy, dieted, making themselves ill and unhealthy. Even today, fashion can make some people dissatisfied with their natural shape.

Materials

The four natural fibres used in making cloth are wool, cotton, silk and linen. Wool is used in the fashion world because it is warm and crease-resistant. Cotton is the most widely used fabric in the world. It is strong, washes well and is made into a variety of cloths like cotton sheeting, corduroy and **muslin**. Silk is woven into a number of different fabrics like satin, **chiffon** and velvet. The strong fibres of the flax plant are used to make linen which is sometimes made into stylish suits.

Many fashionable clothes today are made from artificial **synthetic** materials like rayon. This is made by pulping wood and cotton waste and adding various chemicals. Other synthetic fibres, like nylon and polyester, are made from petroleum, coal and agricultural waste which is mixed with chemicals and then treated with immense heat under pressure. Textile manufacturers are always looking at new combinations of natural and synthetic materials for better quality, washable, non-crease, long-wearing materials. Find out what materials your clothes are made from by looking at the labels.

This illustration shows a sample of the labels found on particular items of clothing. The information on the labels tells the wearer how to wash and dry the garment as different materials need different treatment. Do you recognize any of these labels on your clothes?

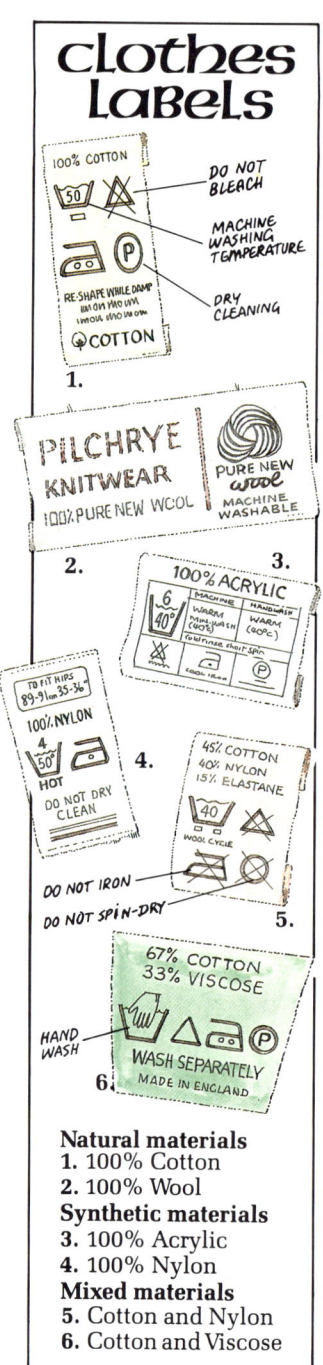

clothes Labels

Natural materials
1. 100% Cotton
2. 100% Wool
Synthetic materials
3. 100% Acrylic
4. 100% Nylon
Mixed materials
5. Cotton and Nylon
6. Cotton and Viscose

Above Wool is a material that never really goes out of fashion. Beautiful jumpers, like this modelled by British actress Sneh Gupta, will never look dated.

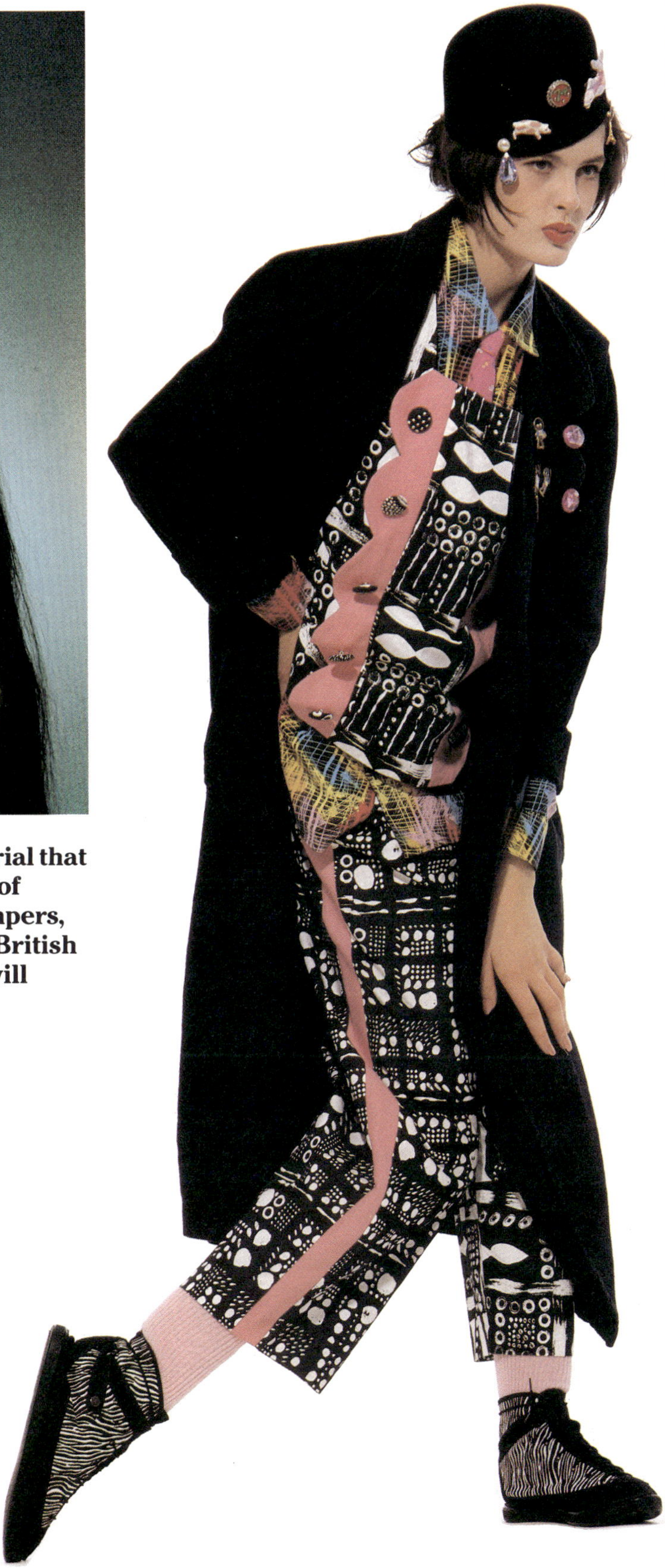

Right Safe fashion is wearing the same kinds of clothes as lots of other people. This model wears clothes that are unusual with striking patterns and colours that make her stand out from the crowd.

Designer Fashion

An Englishman called Charles Frederick Worth was responsible for creating the Parisian system of **haute couture**, or higher dressing, where fashions are displayed on living models. Haute couture is different from other dress businesses because the fashion houses design clothes to suit the looks and personality of each client. There are now fashion centres in Rome, Florence, London, New York as well as Paris, which boast a number of famous names like Jean Muir, Ossie Clark, Jean-Paul Gaultier, Chanel, Dior and Calvin Klein. Rich people wear clothes by their favourite designer at high society events like racing at Ascot, sailing at Cowes Week, at the Cannes film Festival, at Royal weddings and at Oscar ceremonies.

Each season the fashion houses give shows for their rich clients and for the designers from fashion firms and clothes factories who have to pay high prices for the right to copy the new season's styles. The top designers have

Bruce Oldfield is one of the top fashion designers in the world. His clothes are worn by many famous people. Notice how he, like many top designers, does not necessarily wear flamboyant clothes himself.

enormous influence on the silhouette, colour and fabrics for the coming season. They work several seasons ahead and large amounts of money are involved in putting together the new collections. The new styles are kept secret until the moment that the models parade or dance down the **catwalks**. The exotic clothes, the music and the lighting create an exciting atmosphere. Many other accessories like perfume, jewellery and handbags are sold today under designer labels like Gucci and Yves St Laurent.

Above **This model wears a body-hugging, latex dress designed by Jean-Paul Gaultier.**

Left **The changes in men's fashionable clothes are often only a matter of small details.**

Working in Fashion

The world of fashion, or the 'rag trade' as it is sometimes known, is big business and provides thousands of people with jobs. People work in mills manufacturing cloth and in factories dyeing, printing and making it into garments. In some parts of the world, like in the Far East in Taiwan, China and Korea, people work hard for little money. Clothes are mass-produced, often by hand, and exported abroad where they are sold fairly cheaply in high street shops. T-shirts, knitwear and

Behind all the glamour associated with the fashion industry, are the people who work long hours in factories making the clothes.

How long does it take you to get dressed in the morning? Imagine being a model and having to change into a new outfit in two minutes about twenty times in an evening.

appliqué work are produced like this. As well as large, machine-run factories there are smaller 'sweat shops' where workers sit for long hours at sewing machines, sewing up one piece of a garment and then passing it on to the next worker. Dressmakers, tailors, **milliners**, jewellers, shoe makers, **haberdashers**, and **drapers** are some of the other people who work with fashionable clothes. Many people have jobs selling the clothes in boutiques, small clothes shops, large department stores, chain stores and even by mail order.

A smaller number of people work in the more glamorous part of the fashion world. These are the dress designers, models, photographers and hairstylists who work to produce exciting and original fashion shows. The end result is colourful and glamorous but everyone works fast and furiously behind the scenes. Modelling can be fun but also very tiring. Long hours are spent practising for fashion shows or preparing for photography sessions. The most successful models are fit, elegant and well proportioned and can act to suit the different clothes that they model.

Chapter 6

Street Fashion

The latest ideas from the fashion centres of the world influence what the ordinary person wears on the street. Fashion designers always have to think ahead about what will be fashionable the next season, and the next and so on. The shape, colour and fabric of designer clothes are slightly altered to make a cheaper, mass-produced version of the same style that can be sold in high street shops.

The competition at street level to attract

Below This is a selection of typical American street fashion — T-shirts, jeans and trendy baggy shorts.

One kind of street fashion that is popular all over the world is jeans, sweat shirts and bomber jackets.

Clothes and hairstyles that were fashionable in the 1950s — jeans and baseball jackets, for example — have become extremely popular in the 1980s.

customers is very fierce. A great deal of money is spent on research. Information is gathered about people's lifestyles, wealth and tastes. Large firms spend vast sums of money on advertising their new season's looks and high street shop windows are attractively dressed to tempt passing shoppers inside. Many chain stores, like Benetton and Next, display a coordinated look to encourage shoppers to buy whole outfits. These can be up-dated from the small high street shops which specialize in selling accessories like socks and tights, ties, gloves, scarves and jewellery in the latest colours and styles.

Street fashion can sometimes be a sort of uniform when people choose similar colours and styles.

Fashion and the Media

Music and fashion

Pop stars use fashionable clothes skilfully. They need to appear to be at the forefront of fashion, setting the new trends. They need to stand out from the crowd so that they, and therefore their music, appear to be interesting, modern and unusual. Famous pop stars have large followings of fans who copy their style of dressing. This sometimes starts new fashions. One of American rockstar Madonna's 'looks' — black and white lace with black leather, fishnet tights and high-heeled shoes — was copied by teenagers all over the world.

Each different image used by famous stars influences fashions and reflects certain beliefs about lifestyles and behaviour. Groups like the Communards have used skinhead fashion as

Singers Pepsi (right) and Shirley wear a style of dress that has become extremely fashionable. Because they appeared on television and in magazines so much, many people were able to see their clothes, like them and wish to wear them. In fact, so many teenagers copied their clothes that Pepsi and Shirley have designed clothes which are now on sale in high street shops.

Pop stars, like American singer Terence Trent D'Arby, sometimes choose a more formal style of dress when performing on stage.

Fans of pop stars often copy their style of dress. Madonna has set many teenage fashion trends in the 1980s with her different 'looks'.

part of their act. This 'look' is similar to the bovver boys of the 70s who wore braces, high-laced boots and very short hairstyles. Punk fashion was first displayed by bands like the Sex Pistols. The black clothes and hairstyles of either a halo of stiffened spikes or a mohican plume with the sides of the head shaved, in black, blond, brilliant lime greens or shocking pinks, are now familiar sights.

Fans of rock star Bruce Springsteen and rock groups like Kiss, Def Leppard and Marillion have a completely different image of long hair and casual clothes, like jeans and T-shirts. Some bands cultivate a 'boy-next-door' look like A-ha. The Housemartins have a deliberately 'ordinary' appearance unlike pop artists like Boy George and Freddy Mercury who dress in an array of outrageous costumes.

TV and films

Television influences new fashions in clothes. Millions of people watch hours of television every day and it is the major source of public information. People watch their favourite TV stars and then go out and copy their clothes, hairstyles and sometimes their behaviour and lifestyle. Joan Collins and her padded shoulder look and the smartly suited women in the television programme *Dallas*, brought broad-shouldered, pastel-coloured suits into fashion stores worldwide.

Films and videos also influence the way people dress. Films set in particular countries

create different 'looks'. The more exotic clothes tend to get copied. After the films *Out of Africa* and *White Mischief* were released the main street shops were flooded with khaki

Right Raisa Gorbachev, wife of the leader of the USSR, brought the cossack look back into the 1980s.

The clothes worn by TV's *Dynasty* stars affect fashions for older people.

cotton clothes worn with accessories like fake zebra and lion skin belts and pith helmets. After films about India like *Gandhi, A Passage to India* and *Heat and Dust* soft folds and colourful Indian prints became fashionable.

The **cossack** look became all the rage in the 1960s, after the film set in Russia called *Dr. Zhivago*. Today there are many news items on the Russians and their leader Mr Gorbachev, and the cossack look is back. Individual film actresses and actors often have cult followings. James Dean and Marlon Brando created a whole 'anti hero' look in the 1950s, wearing dark leather jackets and casual jeans. This look has made a comeback and is very fashionable today.

James Dean was a popular actor in the 1950s. His moody 'anti hero' look is still fashionable today.

Magazines

For centuries dressmakers in European fashion centres advertised their new styles by dressing little dolls in the latest fashions and sending them to rich clients who copied the outfits. In time, coloured fashion prints were invented and reproduced in quantity. Nowadays, the thousands of fashion magazines that roll off the printing presses and into the newsagents each week play an important part in informing the public about new fashions. The magazines carry huge numbers of advertisements by manufacturers selling the new fashions.

Teenage pop and fashion magazines have an enormous readership amongst teenagers. They are full of advice on new looks as well as pictures and interviews about famous stars and their fashion tastes. Fashion magazines tell us what styles and shapes are currently 'in' and give advice on healthy living. There is advice on make-up and the latest hairstyles. The new **coordinated colours** are discussed and illustrated, and there is even advice about the fashionable ways to behave. Useful information about the latest styles and colours of accessories like shoes, hats, gloves and scarves are often alongside details on how to knit fashionable jumpers or make trendy clothes and jewellery.

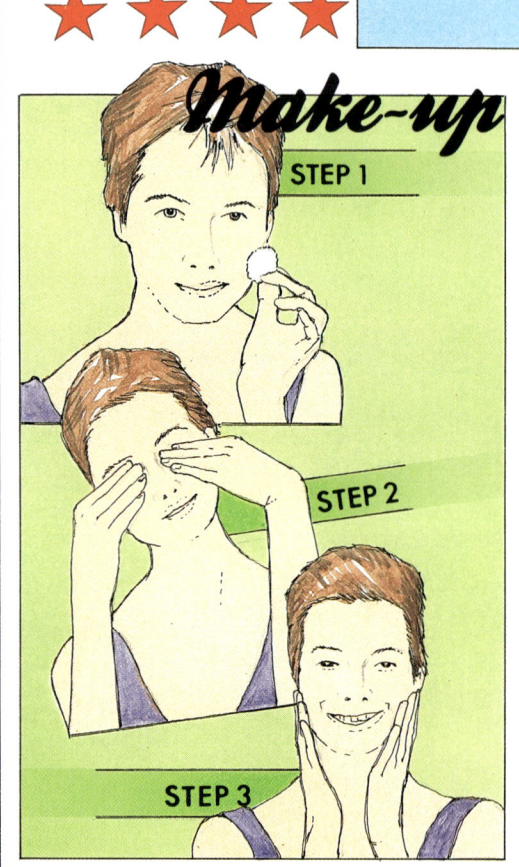

Make-up

STEP 1

STEP 2

STEP 3

T-SHIRT OFFER!

SHORTS

Star talk

★ ★ ★ ★

Fashionable Children

Throughout history, fashionable children were dressed in small versions of adult clothing. Babies in the sixteenth century wore heavily embroidered dresses, a cap and a stiff ruff collar. Early this century boys up to the age of five wore dresses. After this they wore shorts with some American boys wearing long woollen stockings attached to **suspenders** around the waist!

As soon as a baby is born it is a **consumer**. Babies' clothes are no longer made to restrict movement. They wear all-in-one suits of stretchy, washable materials that fasten all the way down the front for easy changing. Toddlers' clothes are also designed in practical styles to suit their active lives. They wear hard-wearing clothes like dungarees. The jumpers and shirts worn underneath are often made from synthetic materials that are easy to clean. Older children's fashionable clothes include tracksuit tops and bottoms, sweat shirts and T-shirts. Teenagers wear fashionable clothes which are very similar to those worn by adults.

Children today have a much greater awareness of fashion, and like to copy the dress sense of people who they admire. Jeans, baseball jackets, jumpers and leggings, or skirts of the latest length are all popular fashions. Hair tiebacks for girls and other accessories like patterned braces, fun buttons and shoe laces, gloves, scarves, hats and multi-coloured watches are all popular in creating a fashionable appearance.

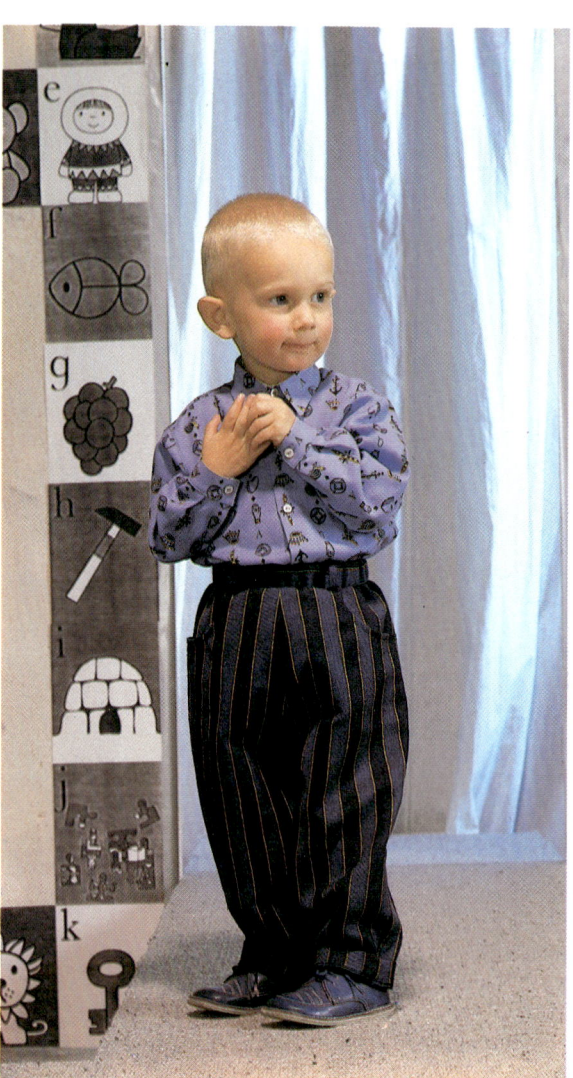

Many parents like to dress their children in trendy clothes. As a result, fashion shows where children of all ages model the latest styles are commonplace. This little boy is wearing a smart shirt and baggy trousers which are miniature versions of adult fashions.

Above These young Australians in Parramatta Park, New South Wales, are wearing clothes that are fashionable amongst young people all over the world — T-shirts, sweat shirts, jeans and shorts.

As younger and younger children become more interested in fashionable clothes, young models like Felix, who appeared in Madonna's *Open Your Heart* video, are becoming famous.

The Denim Revolution

The word denim comes from 'de Nimes' as the fabric was first manufactured in the French town of Nimes. The blue jeans fashion began in the 1850s when Levi Strauss originally made them in tough canvas. Later they were made in denim with the seams strengthened by copper rivets. Denim clothes are now worn all over the world by all ages, by males and females and by both rich and poor.

Jeans and other denim clothes have remained popular and fashionable because they adapt so easily to new fashions and are strong and reliable. The jeans shape often changes. There have been skintight, stretchy,

Ripped, patched and torn jeans have been brought back into fashion in the 1980s.

loose, pleated, baggy, narrow-leg, straight-leg, calf-length, flared, bell-bottomed, high-waisted and hipster jeans. Denim jackets can be hip-hugging, long, cropped and oversize.

Denim fits the many moods of fashion and each new look shows a different attitude to life. Smart designer jeans by Yves St Laurent and Gloria Vanderbilt are worn with elegant silk shirts and ties, and linen or velvet jackets. Expensive designers like Chanel make denim suits and Fabrice make beaded denim gowns.

Denim is stone-washed, bleached and can be worn deliberately crumpled and frayed,

Denim jackets are hard-wearing and comfortable and suit both casual and smart occasions.

Pop star Whitney Houston relaxes offstage in a pair of comfortable, denim jeans.

patched, pre-shrunk, and faded. Casual denim jeans are sometimes worn with denim jackets, tweed jackets or with leather ones decorated with studs, chains and badges. The 'macho' look combines denim and a sweat shirt with the sleeves torn off. Through the years denim has become a sort of 'clothes-language' for young people. They have covered their favourite jeans with bright embroidery, appliqué work, patches, feathers, leather and silk trims, fake jewellery, sequins and even paint. Decorative jeans can almost be considered an art form.

Health and Fashion

Fashionable clothes are very closely connected with people's lifestyles. Healthier living with increased physical fitness is the fashionable way to live today. Many more people have taken up regular exercise in the form of activities like jogging, weightlifting, swimming, or aerobics. The fashion designers and manufacturers have responded to this by producing a whole new range of clothes based on sportswear. The 'total', or complete look, is a healthy, natural one.

Jogging suits, like the traditional tracksuits for athletes, are worn by all ages. They are often made of knitted cotton with a fleecy lining which provides warmth and cover but also complete comfort and freedom of movement. Leggings, leotards and a wide range of bright, lightweight swimwear are all part of this healthy look. Today, many more people can afford to go skiing and street skiwear, like brightly-coloured anoraks with double-lined trousers, are popular. Designers of sportswear now sell their clothes to the general public. Lacoste shirts and jumpers, for example, originally worn by golfing stars, are highly fashionable. The Sloane Rangers image of waxed Barbour coats, pearls, silk scarves and green wellingtons, is one which reflects a wealthy lifestyle and outdoor interests.

The ever-changing world of fashion brings variety, colour and excitement into our lives. In the twenty-first century people will look at photographs of you taken today and laugh at, what will be to them, your funny, old-fashioned clothes.

Left Colourful, comfortable jogging suits are an example of fashionable clothes that have been adapted from sports clothes.

Opposite Both Madonna and her bodyguard jog through Central Park, New York in tight-fitting, lurex cycling shorts and leggings.

Glossary

Appliqué A decoration made by sewing one piece of material on to another.

Bustle A framework worn under the skirt at the back to make it stick out. Fashionable amongst women in the nineteenth century.

Catwalks The narrow pathway over a stage used by fashion models to walk up and down when displaying clothes to an audience.

Chiffon A fine, see-through fabric of silk and nylon.

Consumer A person who buys goods.

Coordinated colours Colours which match together.

Cossacks Originally east Russian warrior peasants who served as mounted soldiers. The style of their fur-trimmed, long, woollen coats and fur hats are often copied.

Crinoline A petticoat stiffened with horsehair and linen, worn under skirts to make them fuller.

Drapers People who sell fabrics and sewing materials.

Empire line Dresses that have a short bodice and long skirt.

Ermine The white fur of a stoat.

Haberdashers People who sell small items to do with sewing like buttons, zips and ribbons.

Haute couture The most expensive fashions.

Leg-o'-mutton The shape of a sleeve which goes from very full at the top to very narrow at the bottom.

Mass-produce To make a large number of goods using machinery.

Media Forms of communicating news and information to the general public — newspapers, music, magazines, television and radio.

Milliners People who make or sell women's hats.

Muslin A fine, plain-weave, cotton fabric.

Panier A hooped framework worn under women's skirts in the nineteenth century.

Puritans People, who in the late sixteenth and seventeenth centuries, held very strict religious and moral principles.

Silhouette An outline drawing of a face or figure, filled in with black.

Sumptuary laws Laws which controlled the amount of money that people could spend on personal items such as clothes.

Suspenders An elastic strap attached to a belt with a fastening at the end.

Synthetic A material that has been made using chemicals.

Women's liberation movement A movement organized to campaign for women to be treated equally with men.

Index

Books to read

A Visual History of Costume: The Twentieth Century by Penelope Byrde [B T Batsford Ltd London, 1986]

Costume Reference 10: 1950 to the Present Day by Marion Sichel [B T Batsford London, 1979]

Costumes and Clothes by Jean Cooke [Wayland (Publishers) Ltd, 1986]

Dress and Fashion by Olive Ordish [Routledge & Kegan Paul Ltd, 1974]

Exploring Clothes by Brenda Ralph Lewis [Wayland (Publishers) Ltd, 1988]

Fashion in the Twentieth Century by Eleanor Van Zandt [Wayland (Publishers) Ltd, 1988]

Just Look at Clothes by Brenda Ralph Lewis [Macdonald Educational, 1986]

The Anatomy of Costume by Robert Selbie [Bell and Hyman Limited, 1982]

Acknowledgements

The Publisher would like to thank the following for providing the pictures used in this book: Barnaby's Picture Library 16 (top); BBC Hulton Picture Library 21; David Bowden 25 (top); Bridgeman Art Library 9 (left); Camera Press 4, 9 (right), 13 (left), 15, 28; London Features International COVER (photographer Mike Prior, courtesy of *Number One* magazine); Penny McDowell 27 (right); Duncan Raban 18, 19 (right), 25 (bottom), 27 (left), 29; David Redfern 19 (left), 26; Syndication International 11 (right); Topham Picture Library 8, 11 (left), 12, 13 (right), 17, 20, 24; Malcolm Walker 7, 22-3; Wayland Picture Library 6; Stephen Wheele 10; John Wright 16 (bottom); ZEFA 5, 14.